SNACKS
& Suppers

There's a certain formality associated with most mealtimes, but snacks and suppers are in a different category altogether! The very word 'snack' implies indulgence; a treat sneaked between meals or a small, speedily-prepared dish for those days when you have neither the energy nor the inclination to make a more elaborate lunch or dinner.

Suppers are somewhat more substantial, but equally casual. Invite guests for dinner, and you immediately start worrying about starters and seating plans; by contrast, a supper invitation suggests a few good friends tucking in to a casserole at the kitchen table.

In this recipe collection you'll find plenty of ideas for all occasions, from snacks to satisfy hungry schoolchildren to sophisticated nibbles to serve with drinks. There are one-dish suppers which can be cooked ahead or speedily assembled at the last minute, late-night pasta and egg dishes which take only minutes to make, plus soups and sandwiches for lazy lunches. Treats on Trays focuses on individual desserts, and you'll find more sweet suggestions, many of them based on fresh fruit, in the chapter devoted to after-school snacks.

CONTENTS

AFTER SCHOOL SNACKS

The door bangs, bags are dropped in the hall, and the cry goes up:
"What is there to eat? We're starving!"
Stave off post-school starvation with this selection of savoury and sweet snacks.

Tuna Fish Fingers

1 x 220g (7oz) can tuna, drained and mashed

2 medium potatoes, boiled and mashed

2 tblspn chopped fresh parsley

1 tblspn soy sauce

1 tblspn chutney

1 egg, beaten

90g (3oz) wholewheat breadcrumbs

1 Combine the tuna, mashed potatoes, parsley, soy sauce and chutney in a bowl. Gradually add enough of the egg to make a moist but not sloppy mixture.

2 Divide the mixture evenly into 10 portions; form each portion into a 1cm (1/2in) thick fish finger.

3 Spread out the breadcrumbs in a shallow bowl. Add the fish fingers and turn them in the crumbs until well coated. Chill on a baking sheet for 30 minutes.

4 Preheat oven to 180°C (350°F/ Gas 4). Bake the tuna fish fingers for 10 minutes or until golden.
Serves 4

Kitchen Tip
If preferred, the fish fingers may be grilled or shallow fried in hot oil.

Sweetcorn and Ham Croquettes

125g (4oz) butter

125g (4oz) plain flour

250ml (8fl oz) milk

250ml (8fl oz) chicken stock

155g (5oz) drained canned or thawed frozen sweetcorn

250g (8oz) cooked ham, chopped

salt

freshly ground black pepper

grated nutmeg

1 egg yolk

2 eggs, beaten

185g (6oz) dried breadcrumbs

oil for deep frying

1 Melt butter in a saucepan, add half the flour and cook for 1 minute. Gradually add milk and stock, stirring until mixture boils and thickens.

2 Stir in corn and chopped ham, with salt, pepper and nutmeg to taste. Cool slightly and stir in egg yolk.

3 Spread mixture in a 20cm (8in) square dish. Cover and chill for about 4 hours until firm.

4 Cut mixture into squares. Dredge in remaining flour, shaking off excess. Dip floured squares in beaten egg, then in breadcrumbs to coat. Deep fry croquettes in hot oil until golden. Drain on paper towels. Serve hot.
Makes 16

Tuna Fish Fingers

Fruity Cheese Log

Toasted Cheese Snack

6 slices brown bread

2 tspn mild mustard

6 slices cooked chicken or chicken roll

125g (4oz) Cheddar cheese, grated

3 tblspn mayonnaise

2 spring onions, finely chopped

1 Toast bread, then spread each slice with a little of the mustard. Top with a slice of chicken or chicken roll.

2 Combine cheese, mayonnaise and spring onions in a bowl; mix well. Spread cheese mixture on top of each chicken slice.

3 Cook under a preheated grill for about 3 minutes, or until cheese mixture bubbles. Serve at once, with a salad garnish if liked.
Serves 3-6

Variations
Not all children like the flavour of mustard; spread the toast with sweet fruit chutney or a thin layer of cranberry jelly instead.

Bubbly Cheese, Ham and Pineapple Toasts

250g (8oz) Red Leicester cheese, grated

90g (3oz) lean cooked ham, chopped

2 eggs, lightly beaten

8 slices wholewheat bread

8 canned pineapple rings

1 Combine cheese and ham in a mixing bowl. Add beaten egg and mix lightly. Set aside.

2 Toast bread slices on one side only under a preheated grill. Turn bread slices over and top each untoasted side with a pineapple ring. Pile cheese mixture on top, spreading it out to cover toast completely.

3 Return toasts to grill until topping is bubbly and golden brown. Serve at once.
Serves 8

Fruity Cheese Log

Make this in advance and keep refrigerated for up to a week.

10 dried apricots, finely chopped

2 tblspn orange juice

1 x 250g (8oz) package cream cheese

60g (2oz) Cheddar cheese, grated

30g (1oz) peanuts, chopped

30g (1oz) poppy seeds

1 Soak apricots in orange juice in a small bowl overnight.

2 Next day, blend cream cheese and Cheddar cheese together in a bowl. Stir in apricot and juice mixture.

3 Add peanuts and mix well. Refrigerate mixture for 1 hour.

4 Shape mixture into a 20cm (8in) log shape; roll in poppy seeds, wrap in greaseproof paper and refrigerate overnight. Serve slices on dry crackers.
Serves 4

Pikelet Faces

155ml (5fl oz) milk

2 tspn grated orange rind

2 tblspn orange juice

3 tblspn oil

60g (2oz) butter, melted

250g (8oz) self-raising flour

1 tblspn cocoa

Honey Butter

60g (2oz) butter, softened

2 tblspn honey

1 Mix milk, orange rind, orange juice and oil in a jug. Stir in half the melted butter.

2 Sift flour into a mixing bowl, make a well in centre and add milk mixture. Stir mixture with a wooden spoon, gradually incorporating flour to make a smooth batter. Alternatively, process ingredients briefly in a blender or food processor.

3 Transfer half the batter to a second bowl; add cocoa and mix until smooth. Spoon cocoa mixture into a piping bag fitted with a plain nozzle.

4 Heat remaining melted butter in a large frying pan (an electric frying pan is ideal). Using chocolate mixture, pipe eyes and mouth shapes onto pan. Leave to cook for 30 seconds. Gently pour 1 tablespoon of the orange pikelet batter on each set of features to make faces. Turn pikelets over when bubbles appear; cook lightly on the other side. Transfer to a wire rack to cool slightly.

5 Mix butter and honey together in a small pot and serve with warm pikelets.
Makes about 20

Sausage Bread Rolls

10 slices bread

4 tblspn fruit chutney or tomato ketchup

5 chipolata sausages, grilled

5 rindless streaky bacon rashers

30g (1oz) butter, melted

1 Preheat oven to 180°C (350°F/ Gas 4). Using a sharp knife, remove the crusts from the bread. Spread each slice with chutney or ketchup.

2 Cut each grilled sausage in half and place diagonally in the centre of a slice of bread. Roll up.

3 Cut each bacon rasher in half lengthwise; roll a bacon strip around the centre of each roll.

4 Brush the bread with the melted butter; place on a baking sheet. Bake for 15 minutes until golden.
Makes 10

Sandwich Selection

Ideal for those occasions when your son or daughter comes home with the entire hockey team.

2 loaves wholemeal bread

softened butter or margarine

fish paste

100g (3 1/2oz) cream cheese

1 tblspn chopped fresh parsley

2 hard-boiled eggs, mashed

2 tspn mayonnaise

salt

freshly ground black pepper

peanut butter

yeast extract

parsley sprigs for garnish

1 Thinly spread the bread slices with butter or margarine. Make four sandwiches with each of the following fillings: fish paste; cream cheese and parsley; egg mixed with mayonnaise (with salt and pepper to taste); peanut butter and yeast extract.

2 Cut off the crusts, if liked. Cut each sandwich into three fingers or four triangles. Arrange on a tray, decorated with parsley sprigs.

Makes 20 sandwiches or 60 fingers or 80 triangles

Sausage Bread Rolls, Pikelet Faces

Battered Layer Sandwiches

These delicious sandwiches are very filling; two quarters make a satisfying snack.

6 slices smoked ham
6 slices Gruyére cheese
6 slices cooked turkey
12 thick slices white bread, crusts removed
oil for deep frying
cranberry sauce to serve

Batter

500ml (16fl oz) milk
2 tspn lemon juice
2 eggs, beaten
½ tspn bicarbonate of soda
220g (7oz) plain flour
1½ tblspn sunflower oil
1 tblspn baking powder
½ tspn salt
¼ tspn vanilla essence

1 Make batter. Mix milk and lemon juice in a jug. Leave to stand for 10 minutes, then pour into a blender or food processor. Add eggs and bicarbonate of soda and blend. Add remaining batter ingredients; blend until smooth. Refrigerate for 1 hour.

2 Make six sandwiches, each consisting of a layer of ham, cheese and turkey between 2 slices of bread. Cut each sandwich into four squares. Secure layers firmly with a cocktail stick.

3 Dip sandwiches in batter to coat on all sides. Deep fry in hot oil in batches until golden, about 3 minutes. Drain on paper towels. Serve hot with cranberry sauce for dipping.
Makes 24

Variation
Offer a selection of dipping sauces for greater variety. Mayonnaise mixed with mild mustard; natural low-fat yogurt mixed with tomato purée or a hot home-made tomato sauce are all suitable.

Flatbread Pizza

Flatbread Pizza

2 rounds of flatbread

2 tblspn tomato purée

125g (4oz) cooked ham, chopped

125g (4oz) Cheddar cheese, grated

1 tblspn chopped fresh parsley

1 Preheat oven to 180°C (350°F/Gas 4). Spread each flatbread round thinly with tomato purée. Sprinkle ham, cheese and parsley on top.

2 Bake for 15 minutes. Serve in wedges.

Makes 8 wedges

Variations
Add any of the following, or a combination: crumbled grilled bacon, lightly cooked sliced mushrooms, sliced pepperoni sausage, drained canned sweetcorn, drained canned tuna flakes, red, green or yellow pepper strips lightly fried in oil.

Toasted Sandwiches with Corn, Egg or Tuna

Expecting a crowd? Make up a batch of sandwiches with a choice of fillings and toast them to order.

60 slices white sandwich bread

30 cheese slices

softened butter for spreading

Corn Filling

200g (6½ oz) Cheddar cheese, grated

315g (10oz) canned cream-style sweetcorn

Egg Filling

5 hard-boiled eggs, chopped

125g (4oz) grated Red Leicester cheese

Tuna Filling

1 x 440g (14oz) can tuna in oil, drained and flaked

60ml (2fl oz) mayonnaise

1 Corn Filling. Combine the grated Cheddar cheese and sweetcorn in a bowl. Mix thoroughly.

2 Egg Filling. Mix the chopped eggs and Red Leicester cheese in a second bowl.

3 Tuna Filling. Tip the tuna into a third bowl, mash lightly and mix with the mayonnaise.

4 Top ten slices of bread with each filling. Add a slice of cheese to each and complete each sandwich with a bread slice. Spread the top of each sandwich lightly with butter.

5 Preheat a toasted sandwich maker. Add the sandwiches, butter side down, then lightly butter the sides that are uppermost. Cook for 2-3 minutes or until golden. If necessary, keep each batch of sandwiches hot while cooking the next.

Makes 30

Date Crumbcake

| 155g (5oz) butter, softened |
| 155g (5oz) sugar |
| 4 eggs |
| 140g (4¹/₂oz) plain flour |
| 1 tspn baking powder |
| 1 tspn vanilla essence |
| 125g (4oz) sugar-rolled chopped dates |

Crumb Topping

| 125g (4oz) butter, diced |
| 125g (4oz) soft light brown sugar |
| 125g (4oz) plain flour |
| 1 tspn cinnamon |

1 Set oven to 180°C (350°F/Gas 4). Butter a 20cm (8in) deep square cake tin. Line base of tin with nonstick baking parchment.

2 Cream butter with sugar in a mixing bowl until light and fluffy. Add eggs, one at a time, beating after each addition and adding a little of the flour if mixture shows sign of curdling. Add flour and baking powder; mix well. Beat in the vanilla essence.

3 Spoon mixture into prepared tin, level surface and sprinkle dates on top, leaving a 2.5cm (1in) border around the outside. Bake for 20 minutes.

4 Meanwhile make crumb topping. Combine butter, sugar, flour and cinnamon in a food processor; pulse several times until mixture resembles coarse breadcrumbs. Alternatively, mix dry ingredients in a bowl and rub in butter.

5 After 20 minutes' baking, remove cake from oven and sprinkle crumb topping evenly on top. Return to oven for 30 minutes more, or until a skewer inserted in cake comes out clean. The topping will not be crunchy at this stage.

6 Cool in tin for 1 hour, then transfer cake to a wire rack, crumb side up, and cool to room temperature. Serve in squares.
Makes 16 squares

Berry and Yogurt Jellies

| 1 packet or tablet raspberry jelly |
| 100g (3¹/₂oz) fresh or frozen raspberries |
| 155ml (5fl oz) raspberry yogurt |

1 Make jelly according to packet instructions. Cool slightly.

2 Add raspberries and yogurt; mix well. Pour jelly into four serving dishes. Chill until set.
Serves 4

Jelly Oranges

| 3 oranges |
| 1 packet or tablet orange jelly |
| 375ml (12fl oz) boiling water |

1 Cut oranges in half. Squeeze juice, taking care not to damage skins. Set aside 125ml (4fl oz) of orange juice. Scoop out and discard any pulp remaining in orange halves, keeping them intact.

2 Dissolve jelly in boiling water. Stir in reserved orange juice. Cool, then chill for 30 minutes or until on the point of setting.

3 Arrange clean orange halves on a tray, using crumpled foil if necessary to keep them upright. Fill skins with orange jelly and refrigerate until set. Just before serving, slice the jelly oranges into quarters.
Makes 12

Frozen Banana Lollies

| 5 just-ripe bananas |
| 10 lolly sticks |
| 125g (4oz) dark chocolate, in squares |
| 125g (4oz) peanuts or almonds, finely chopped |

1 Line two baking sheets with baking parchment. Peel the bananas and cut them in half. Insert a lolly stick into each half.

2 Melt the chocolate in a heatproof bowl over hot water.

3 Brush each banana generously with chocolate, roll in the chopped nuts and arrange on the prepared baking sheets. Freeze, covered, until firm.
Makes 10

Frozen Banana Lollies

Oat Bran Biscuits

125g (4oz) self-raising flour
2 tblspn custard powder
75g (2½oz) soft light brown sugar
60g (2oz) rolled oats
30g (1oz) dry oat bran
155g (5oz) butter, chopped
2 tblspn honey

1 Preheat oven to 180°C (350°F/ Gas 4). Grease 2 baking sheets. Sift the flour and custard powder into a bowl. Add the sugar, oats and bran; mix well. Rub in the butter until the mixture resembles coarse crumbs. Stir in the honey.

2 Roll teaspoonfuls of the mixture into balls. Place the balls on the prepared baking sheets, leaving about 3cm (1¼in) between each.

3 Press each biscuit down lightly with a fork. Bake for about 15 minutes. Cool on a wire rack.
Makes about 25

Fudge Peanut Delights

60g (2oz) butter
90g (3oz) soft light brown sugar
125ml (4fl oz) evaporated milk
125g (4oz) white chocolate, chopped
185g (6oz) crunchy peanut butter
220g (7oz) rolled oats
90g (3oz) desiccated coconut
15 glacé cherries

1 Melt the butter, without allowing it to boil, in a large saucepan. Add the sugar and evaporated milk and stir constantly, without boiling, until the sugar has dissolved. Raise the heat and boil for 3 minutes, stirring constantly.

2 Add the chocolate and peanut butter, stirring until the chocolate has melted. Off the heat, stir in the oats and coconut.

Oat Bran Biscuits, Fudge Peanut Delights

3 Drop teaspoonfuls of mixture into paper cupcake cases. Top each Fudge Peanut Delight with half a glacé cherry and refrigerate for about an hour or until set.
Makes about 30

Wholemeal Apricot Slice

185g (6oz) wholemeal flour
125g (4oz) plain flour
125g (4oz) butter
60ml (2fl oz) milk
1 egg, lightly beaten
1 tblspn honey
250g (8oz) dried apricots, chopped
375ml (12fl oz) water
1 tblspn grated orange rind
60ml (2fl oz) orange juice
30g (1oz) caster sugar
1 egg white
2 tblspn caster sugar

1 Preheat oven to 190°C (375°F/Gas 5). Sift the flours into a large mixing bowl, returning the husks from the wholemeal flour to the bowl. Rub in the butter, then stir in the milk, egg and honey to make a soft dough.

2 Knead the dough on a lightly floured surface until smooth. Roll out half the dough to fit a greased Swiss roll tin.

3 Combine the apricots, water, orange rind, juice and sugar in a saucepan. Bring to the boil, stirring. Lower the heat and simmer until the apricots are soft. Process briefly in a food processor; the apricots should be roughly chopped, not puréed. Cool to room temperature.

4 Spread the filling over the pastry. Roll out the remaining pastry to cover. Brush the slice lightly with egg white; sprinkle with caster sugar. Bake for 10 minutes, then lower the oven temperature to 170°C (325°F/Gas 3) and bake for 20 minutes more. Cool in the tin. Cut into bars when cold.
Makes about 20 bars

Angel Food Cake

12 large egg whites
1 tspn cream of tartar
pinch of salt
375g (12oz) caster sugar
155g (5oz) plain flour
1 tspn vanilla essence
½ tspn almond essence
½ tspn lemon juice

1 Preheat oven to 150°C (300°F/ Gas 2). Combine egg whites, cream of tartar and salt in a large grease-free mixing bowl. Beat until soft peaks form. Sprinkle 2 tablespoons of sugar over surface and gently fold in to egg whites. Continue in this manner until all the sugar has been incorporated.

2 Sprinkle 2 tablespoons of flour over surface and gently fold in to mixture. Continue in same way until all the flour has been added.

3 Sprinkle vanilla essence, almond essence and lemon juice over surface of mixture and gently fold in.

4 Spoon batter into an ungreased 25 x 11cm (10 x 4½in) tube tin or angel food cake tin. Bake for 1 hour 10 minutes, or until top of cake springs back when pressed.

Remove from oven and carefully run a knife around edges to loosen cake. Invert tin onto a wire rack. Allow cake to cool completely before removing it from tin.

5 Serve in slices, with thick cream or Greek yogurt and any kind of berries.
Serves 12

Fresh Strawberry Trifle

185g (6oz) bought sponge cake
strawberry jam for spreading
2 tblspn sherry (optional)
250g (8oz) strawberries, halved or quartered
250ml (8fl oz) whipping cream

Custard

600ml (1pt) milk
4 egg yolks
1½ tspn cornflour
2 tblspn caster sugar
½ tspn vanilla essence
freshly grated rind of ½ lemon

1 Make custard. Heat milk in a medium saucepan. Combine egg yolks, cornflour, caster sugar, vanilla essence and lemon rind in a bowl. Beat well until combined. Pour a little of hot milk onto egg yolk mixture, beat well, then pour this mixture into the hot milk. Stir over gentle heat until custard thickens sufficiently to coat back of spoon thickly. Cover custard with dampened greaseproof paper and set aside to cool.

2 Place cake in a glass bowl. Spread surface with strawberry jam and sprinkle with sherry, if used. Top with strawberries. Pour the cool custard over the top.

3 Whip cream until it just holds its shape. Spoon cream over custard. Refrigerate until ready to serve.
Serves 6-8

Fruit Kebabs

You will need 12 wooden or metal skewers to make the kebabs.

1 small pineapple
2 kiwi fruits
250g (8oz) large strawberries

Dressing

1 tblspn lemon juice
2 tblspn orange juice
1 tblspn honey
1 tblspn grated orange rind

1 Peel and core pineapple; cut into 2.5cm (1in) cubes. Peel and quarter kiwi fruit. Hull strawberries. Thread fruit alternately onto skewers.

2 Make dressing by combining all ingredients in a small bowl. Beat well. Brush a little of dressing over the kebabs.

3 Grill kebabs under a hot grill or over hot coals, turning frequently, until hot. Baste frequently with dressing while cooking.
Makes 12

Fruit Kebabs

Strawberry and Mango Salad with Honey Cream

Apricot Yogurt Freeze

375g (12oz) apricot jam

250ml (8fl oz) low fat plain yogurt

90g (3oz) powdered milk

2 egg whites

1 Combine jam, yogurt and powdered milk in a blender or food processor. Process for 1 minute, then scrape the mixture into a large bowl. Set aside.

2 Beat egg whites in a large grease-free bowl until stiff. Gently fold into apricot mixture.

3 Spoon into a 20 x 10cm (8 x 4in) loaf tin. Freeze until firm. Serve thinly sliced.
Serves 4

Banana Whip

As the eggs in this sweet snack are not cooked, it is vital that they be both very fresh and purchased from a reliable source.

2 egg whites

2 tblspn sugar

1 large banana, mashed

2 tblspn lemon juice

1 tspn cocoa

1 Beat egg whites in a large grease-free bowl until stiff. Fold in sugar. Fold banana into mixture, with lemon juice and cocoa.

2 Divide banana whip between four individual dessert dishes. Serve at once.
Serves 4

Strawberry and Mango Salad with Honey Cream

250g (8oz) strawberries

2 mangoes

1 tblspn honey

125ml (4fl oz) soured cream or fromage frais

1 Cut the strawberries and mango flesh into 2cm (3/4in) cubes. Arrange in four individual dessert dishes.

2 Combine honey and soured cream or fromage frais in a bowl. Mix well. Spoon cream mixture over fruit. Chill before serving.
Serves 4

TREATS ON TRAYS

Whether you are watching Wimbledon on the small screen or sitting snugly in front of the fire on a wintry evening, soup, sandwiches and easy-to-eat desserts make perfect lap-top treats.

Carrot Soup with Coriander

60g (2oz) butter

4 spring onions, finely chopped

4 tblspn chopped fresh coriander

1 litre (1³/4pt) chicken stock

1 tspn coarsely ground black pepper

500g (1lb) carrots, chopped

1 large potato, chopped

60ml (2fl oz) double cream

3 tblspn chopped fresh parsley

1 Melt the butter in a large saucepan over moderate heat. Add the spring onions and coriander and cook for 2 minutes, shaking the pan frequently to prevent scorching.

2 Add the stock, pepper, carrots and potato. Bring to the boil, then lower the heat and simmer the soup for 20 minutes or until the vegetables are tender.

3 Purée the vegetables and stock in a blender or food processor until smooth. Return the soup to the clean saucepan and heat through.

4 Ladle into heated soup bowls. Drizzle a tablespoonful of cream into each portion, sprinkle with chopped parsley and serve at once, with crusty bread or one of the sandwiches on page 16.
Serves 4

Kitchen Tip
When time is short, grate the carrots and potatoes for speedy cooking.

Beggar's Soup

1 French bread stick, cut into thin slices

1 clove garlic, halved

1 litre (1³/4pt) good-quality chicken stock

185g (6oz) broccoli florets

60g (2oz) grated Parmesan cheese

1 Toast the bread on both sides. Rub the cut side of the garlic generously over each slice of toast.

2 Bring the chicken stock to the boil in a large saucepan. Add the broccoli and cook for 30 seconds.

3 Ladle the soup into heated soup bowls, place two or three slices of garlic toast in each and sprinkle with Parmesan.
Serves 4

Variations
Use thinly sliced button mushrooms instead of the broccoli. Add 1 teaspoon of mushroom ketchup to the chicken stock. Substitute garlic croûtons - bread cubes cooked in garlic butter until crisp - for the garlic toasts.

Beggar's Soup (left), Carrot Soup with Coriander

Pimiento Soup

Hasty Mushroom Soup

60g (2oz) butter

1 onion, roughly chopped

500g (1lb) mushrooms, sliced

1 litre (1³/₄pt) chicken stock

3 egg yolks

salt

freshly ground black pepper

double cream and finely snipped chives for garnish

1 Melt butter in a large saucepan. Add onion and cook for 3-5 minutes until soft. Add mushrooms. Cook over moderate to high heat, stirring, for 4 minutes. Stir in stock and bring to boil.

2 Transfer mushroom mixture to a blender or food processor. Purée, then return to clean saucepan. Heat through gently.

3 Beat egg yolks together in a small bowl. Beat in about 125ml (4fl oz) of mushroom purée, then gradually pour mixture into pan, stirring constantly. Do not boil.

4 Add salt and pepper. Serve, garnishing each portion with cream and chives.

Serves 6-8

Egg Ribbon Soup

45g (1¹/₂oz) fresh breadcrumbs

60g (2oz) grated Parmesan cheese

¹/₂ tspn freshly ground black pepper

pinch of grated nutmeg

3 eggs, lightly beaten

1.2 litres (1³/₄pt) chicken stock

fresh coriander leaves for garnish

1 Combine breadcrumbs, Parmesan, pepper and nutmeg in a bowl. Stir in beaten eggs.

2 Bring chicken stock to boil in a large saucepan. Reduce heat to low. Gradually add breadcrumb mixture, stirring constantly. Cover pan; simmer for 5 minutes more. Serve with a garnish of coriander leaves.

Serves 6

Pimiento Soup

60g (2oz) butter

2 leeks, white part only, sliced

2 cloves garlic, crushed

2 x 440g (14oz) cans pimientos, drained and chopped

2 tblspn tomato purée

500ml (16fl oz) chicken stock

250ml (8fl oz) natural low fat yogurt

125ml (4fl oz) double cream

1 Melt butter in a large saucepan over moderate heat. Add leeks and garlic and sauté for 3-5 minutes until softened but not browned.

2 Stir in pimientos, tomato purée and chicken stock. Bring to boil, lower heat and simmer soup for 20 minutes. Set aside to cool to room temperature.

3 Purée soup in a blender or food processor until smooth. Transfer to a bowl, stir in yogurt and cream, cover and chill for 3 hours before serving.

Serves 4

Minestrone

220g (7oz) cannellini beans, soaked overnight in water to cover

125ml (4fl oz) olive oil

30g (1oz) butter

4 large onions, sliced

2 leeks, sliced

3 carrots, chopped

3 potatoes, cubed

1 stick celery, sliced

125g (4oz) French beans, cut into 2.5cm (1in) pieces

2 courgettes, sliced

45g (1½oz) Savoy cabbage, shredded

1.5-2 litres (2½-3½pt) beef stock

1 tblspn chopped fresh parsley

1 tspn crumbled sage

100g (3½oz) Arborio rice

1 x 397g (13oz) can chopped tomatoes with basil

salt

freshly ground black pepper

60g (2oz) freshly grated Parmesan cheese

1 Drain beans, rinse them in fresh water and drain again. Transfer to a large saucepan with water to cover. Bring to boil, boil for 10 minutes, then lower heat and simmer until tender, about 40 minutes. Drain and set aside.

2 Heat oil and butter together in a large saucepan. Add onions and leeks and sauté until golden. Stir in carrots and sauté for 2 minutes more. Add remaining fresh vegetables in the same way, sautéing each variety for 2 minutes before adding the next.

3 Add 1.5 litres (2½pt) of stock. Stir in parsley and sage. Bring to boil, then lower heat and simmer, covered, for 1 hour, stirring occasionally. Add remaining stock if soup becomes too thick.

4 Add rice, tomatoes and reserved beans, with salt and pepper to taste. Cook until rice is tender. Just before serving, stir in the grated Parmesan.

Serves 6-8

Potato Soup with Croûtons

45g (1½oz) butter

1 onion, chopped

2 cloves garlic, crushed

4 large potatoes, chopped

1 leek, sliced

750ml (1¼pt) chicken stock

½ tspn grated nutmeg

250ml (8fl oz) single cream

oil for shallow frying

4 slices thick white bread, crusts removed, cut into small strips

snipped chives for garnish

1 Melt butter in a large saucepan over moderate heat. Add onion and garlic and cook for 3-5 minutes until softened. Add potatoes, leek slices, chicken stock and nutmeg. Simmer for 20 minutes, or until vegetables are tender.

2 Purée soup, in batches, in a blender or food processor. Return soup to clean saucepan. Stir in cream and mix well. Heat through without boiling.

3 Meanwhile, heat oil in a large frying pan over moderate heat. Add bread strips and cook for 2 minutes, turning frequently. Drain on paper towels. Serve soup in heated bowls, garnished with the croûtons and chives.

Serves 4

Potato Soup with Croûtons

Special Occasion Sandwiches

90g (3oz) smoked salmon (offcuts are ideal)

250g (8oz) cream cheese, softened

2 spring onions, finely chopped

1/2 clove garlic, crushed

2 tblspn chopped fresh parsley

1 tblspn snipped chives

18 slices white sandwich bread

1 Combine smoked salmon with half the cream cheese in a blender or food processor. Purée until smooth. Scrape into a bowl.

2 Place remaining cream cheese in clean food processor or blender. Add spring onions, garlic, parsley and chives. Process until mixture is smooth. Transfer to a second bowl. Cover both bowls and refrigerate for 2 hours or until firm.

3 Cut off crusts from bread slices. Spread six slices with smoked salmon mixture and six slices with herb mixture. Assemble triple decker sandwiches by placing one herb bread slice on top of each smoked salmon bread slice, adding a plain bread slice on top.

4 Cut each sandwich into four triangles. Serve immediately or refrigerate, covered with a damp cloth, for up to 4 hours.
Makes 24 triangles

Red Pepper Sandwiches

125g (4oz) butter, softened

125g (4oz) cream cheese, softened

185g (6oz) red peppers, seeded and roughly chopped

1/4 tspn cayenne pepper

salt

18 slices white sandwich bread

24 black olive slices for garnish

1 Combine butter, cream cheese, red peppers and cayenne in a blender or food processor. Purée until smooth. Scrape into a bowl, add salt to taste, cover and refrigerate until firm, preferably overnight.

2 Cut off crusts from bread slices. Spread 12 slices with red pepper mixture. Assemble triple decker sandwiches by placing two slices topped with red pepper on top of each other, and adding a plain slice on top.

3 Cut each sandwich into four triangles. Serve immediately or refrigerate, covered with a damp cloth, for up to 4 hours.
Makes 24 triangles

Dainty Open Sandwiches

loaves of French bread

softened butter

Suggested Fillings
smoked turkey slices with cranberry jelly, sliced roast beef with bearnaise sauce, sliced hard-boiled egg and caviar, peeled cooked king prawns and mango chutney, tomato, avocado and chopped grilled bacon, smoked salmon with Camembert cheese, sliced salami, cheese and gherkins, ham and asparagus

Garnishes
lettuce, olives, cherry tomatoes, lemon slices, cress, basil, mild onion rings, fresh herbs (chives, basil, parsley, rosemary, dill), strawberries, orange segments, beansprouts

Slice the French bread thinly. Lightly butter one side of each slice. Add any of the suggested toppngs – or invent toppings of your own. Garnish as desired.

Kitchen Tips
These sandwiches should be assembled just before serving. Have the bread buttered and covered, and prepare the ingredients ahead of time, placing them in covered containers in the refrigerator. Any type of bread may be used; the best being the firmer varieties such as rye and pumpernickel, which are easy to pick up and eat. Use sauces, herb butters and mayonnaise to ensure that the toppings adhere to the bread.

Dainty Open Sandwiches

Heart Shapes with Passionfruit Sauce

2 egg whites
440ml (14fl oz) Greek yogurt
caster sugar to taste

Passionfruit Sauce

75g (2¹/₂oz) sugar
freshly squeezed juice of ¹/₂ lemon
10 passionfruit

1 Whisk egg whites in a large grease-free bowl until stiff. Fold in yogurt, then add caster sugar to taste. Line four individual heart-shaped moulds (the type with drainage holes in the bottom) with damp cheesecloth. Divide the yogurt mixture between them. Place moulds on a plate and leave to drain in refrigerator overnight.

2 To make sauce, dissolve the sugar in 75ml (2¹/₂fl oz) water in a saucepan over low heat. Bring to boil, remove from heat and pour syrup into a bowl. Stir in lemon juice.

3 Cut passionfruit in half. Scoop out pulp into a blender or food processor. Process for 15 seconds; just long enough to detach yellow membranes from seeds. Rub through a sieve, pressing out all juice. Mix into syrup. Allow to cool to room temperature, then cover and refrigerate.

4 Turn hearts out onto four dessert plates. Pour passionfruit sauce around hearts and serve at once.
Serves 4

Kitchen Tip
If you do not have the correct moulds, make holes in the bottoms of clean yogurt pots and use them instead.

Blackberry Mousse

500g (1lb) fresh or frozen blackberries
90g (3oz) caster sugar
2 tblspn lemon juice
2 tspn grated lemon rind
2¹/₂ tspn gelatine
3 tblspn water
185ml (6fl oz) double cream
2 egg whites

Decoration

whipped cream, fresh blackberries and mint sprigs

1 Place blackberries in a saucepan over moderate heat. Stir in 60g (2oz) of sugar, with lemon juice and rind. Heat gently, stirring, for 10 minutes.

2 Press mixture through a sieve into a bowl; return to saucepan. Sprinkle gelatine on top of water in a small bowl. When spongy, add to blackberry mixture and dissolve over low heat, stirring. Do not boil. Remove from heat and cool to room temperature.

3 In a bowl, beat cream until soft peaks form. Fold into cooled blackberry mixture.

4 Beat egg whites with remaining sugar in a large grease-free bowl until fluffy; fold in to the blackberry cream. Spoon mixture into four individual serving glasses. Chill until set.

5 Decorate each mousse with a swirl of whipped cream, one or two fresh blackberries and a sprig of mint.
Serves 4

Blackberry Mousse

Chocolate Sienna Cake

Chocolate Sienna Cake

125g (4oz) macadamia nuts, chopped

125g (4oz) walnuts, chopped

125g (4oz) almonds, chopped

155g (5oz) chopped dates

185g (6oz) sultanas

3 tblspn desiccated coconut

60g (2oz) plain flour

60g (2oz) cocoa

75g (2¹/₂oz) icing sugar, plus extra for dusting

250g (8oz) milk chocolate, grated

60g (2oz) butter

185g (6oz) apricot jam

icing sugar for decoration

1 Preheat oven to 180°C (350°F/ Gas 4). Base line and grease a 23cm (9in) flan tin. Combine the nuts, dates, sultanas, coconut, flour, cocoa and icing sugar in a large bowl; set aside.

2 Stir chocolate, butter and jam together in a medium saucepan over low heat until melted; mix well. Pour into the fruit mixture and mix well, using a metal spoon.

3 Spoon the mixture into the prepared tin, pressing it well into the corners. Bake for 35 minutes. Cool in the tin, then transfer to a serving plate, dust with icing sugar and serve.
Serves 10-12

Mocha Hazelnut Meringues

125g (4oz) hazelnuts, chopped

4 egg whites

1 tspn vanilla essence

¹/₈ tspn cream of tartar

75g (2¹/₂oz) icing sugar

1¹/₂ tblspn cocoa

1 tblspn instant coffee dissolved in 2 tspn boiling water

1 Preheat oven to 180°C (350°F/ Gas 4). Spread the hazelnuts on a baking sheet and toast in the oven for about 10 minutes or until golden. Cool. Set aside. Lower the oven temperature to 110°C (225°F/ Gas ¹/₄).

2 In a large grease-free bowl, beat the egg whites until soft peaks form. Add the vanilla and cream of tartar. Continue to beat the mixture, adding the sugar and cocoa little by little, until stiff peaks form. Add the coffee and beat well to incorporate.

3 Stir in the toasted hazelnuts. Drop heaped teaspoonfuls of the mixture onto a baking sheet lined with nonstick baking parchment. Bake for 1 hour.

4 Switch off heat. Leave meringues in oven for 5 minutes, then cool on wire racks. Store in an airtight container.
Makes about 40

CANAPÉS AND COCKTAILS

Mouthwatering morsels, delicious drinks – just add guests for a perfect party. All the canapés in this chapter can be prepared in advance, ready for cooking or simply assembling at the last minute.

Smoked Salmon Cucumber Bites

60g (2oz) smoked salmon
250g (8oz) cream cheese, softened
2 tblspn double cream
2 tspn lemon juice
few drops Tabasco sauce
2 cucumbers
1 lemon
1/4 red pepper, seeded and chopped

1 Combine salmon, cream cheese, cream, lemon juice and Tabasco in a blender or food processor. Purée until smooth. Spoon into a piping bag fitted with a large star nozzle.

2 Cut the cucumbers into 5mm (1/4in) slices. Pipe salmon mixture onto slices and garnish with tiny lemon wedges and pieces of red pepper.
Makes about 36

Avocado Canapés

1 large ripe avocado, halved, stoned and peeled
1 tblspn chopped fresh coriander
1 tblspn lemon juice
2 spring onions, finely chopped
salt
8 rindless streaky bacon rashers
12 slices of pumpernickel, halved
butter, softened

1 Combine avocado, coriander and lemon juice in a bowl. Mash roughly with a fork. Add spring onions, with salt to taste. Cover closely and refrigerate for up to 1 hour.

2 Fry the bacon until crisp. Drain on paper towels. Cut each rasher into three pieces.

3 Spread avocado mixture onto pumpernickel slices, topping each with a piece of bacon.
Makes 24

Almond and Cheese Coated Grapes

125g (4oz) flaked almonds
125g (4oz) cream cheese
60g (2oz) Roquefort or Stilton cheese
2 tblspn double cream
250g (8oz) large seedless green grapes

1 Preheat oven to 180°C (350°F/ Gas 4). Toast almonds on a baking sheet until light golden brown. Chop finely by hand; spread out on a sheet of foil.

2 Beat cream cheese, Roquefort or Stilton and cream in a bowl with an electric hand-held mixer until smooth.

3 Stir grapes into cheese mixture until well covered, then roll them in nuts to coat. Refrigerate until firm.
Makes about 30

Almond and Cheese Coated Grapes

Prawn Toasts

Crostini

Use a seeded loaf, such as a crusty bloomor coated in poppyseeds, to make these tasty titbits.

12 thin slices bread, toasted, halved

3 tblspn anchovy paste or Gentleman's Relish

24 small slices Mozzarella

24 small slices prosciutto

24 slices tomato

60g (2oz) butter

1 tblspn chopped fresh basil

Preheat oven to 180°C (350°F/ Gas 4). Spread toast slices evenly with anchovy paste. Arrange on baking sheets. Top with Mozzarella, prosciutto and tomato. Dot with butter and sprinkle with basil. Bake until cheese starts to melt. Serve at once.

Makes 24

Prawn Toasts

500g (1lb) peeled cooked prawns, deveined

6 spring onions, chopped

2 tspn grated fresh root ginger

2 tspn light soy sauce

1/2 tspn sesame oil

2 egg whites

6 slices white bread

30g (1oz) fresh white breadcrumbs

oil for deep frying

1 Combine prawns, spring onions, ginger, soy sauce and sesame oil in a blender or food processor. Blend until roughly chopped. Add egg whites; blend until combined.

2 Remove crusts from bread slices, spread them with prawn mixture, then cut each slice into three strips.

3 Dip prawn-coated side of each bread strip into breadcrumbs. Deep fry bread strips in hot oil until light golden brown. Drain on paper towels and serve at once, with a coriander garnish, if liked.

Makes 18

Mushrooms Stuffed with Pâté

4 rindless streaky bacon rashers

50 button mushrooms

juice of 1 lemon

250g (8oz) good-quality liver pâté, softened

1 Grill the bacon until crisp. Cool slightly, crumble and set aside.

2 Discard mushroom stems. Wipe caps with a clean damp cloth; sprinkle with the lemon juice.

3 Stuff mushrooms with the pâté, spooning it in or using a piping bag fitted with a plain nozzle. Arrange on a serving platter. Just before serving, sprinkle mushrooms with crumbled bacon.
Makes 50

Pink Lady

60ml (2fl oz) dry white vermouth

30ml (1fl oz) créme de cassis

ice cubes

soda water

Pour vermouth and créme de cassis into a tall glass three quarters filled with ice cubes. Fill up with soda water. Stir gently.
Makes 1

Cherry Cocktail

45ml (1½fl oz) cherry brandy

30ml (1fl oz) brandy

dash Curacao

dash grenadine

dash lemon juice

Combine all ingredients in a cocktail shaker. Shake and pour into a cocktail glass.
Makes 1

Sweet Campari

30ml (1fl oz) Campari

60ml (2fl oz) sweet vermouth

ice cubes

strip of lemon rind

soda water

Pour Campari and vermouth into a tall glass three quarters filled with ice cubes. Add lemon rind, fill with soda water. Stir gently.
Makes 1

Orange Velvet Cocktail

500ml (16fl oz) cognac

250ml (8fl oz) Drambuie

Combine cognac and Drambuie in a large jug. Mix. Serve in liqueur glasses at room temperature.
Makes about 15

Sweet Manhattan

45ml (1½fl oz) whisky

1 tblspn sweet vermouth

dash angostura bitters

ice cubes

1 maraschino cherry

Combine whisky, vermouth and bitters in a jug half filled with ice cubes. Stir, then strain into a cocktail glass. Decorate with cherry.
Makes 1

Kir

30ml (2fl oz) créme de cassis

champagne

Pour créme de cassis into a wine glass. Fill with champagne. Stir gently and serve.
Makes 1

Champagne Cocktail

125ml (4fl oz) orange juice

125ml (4fl oz) lemon juice

750ml (1¼pt) champagne

Mix juices in a jug. Divide between four glasses and fill with champagne.
Serves 4

Champagne Cocktail

23

Avocado Puffs

Choux Pastry

60g (2oz) plain flour

1/4 tspn salt

125ml (4fl oz) water

60g (2oz) butter

2 large eggs

Avocado Filling

2 avocados, halved, stoned, peeled and cubed

2 tblspn lemon juice

1 tblspn chopped onion

salt

cayenne pepper

1 Preheat oven to 200°C (400°F/ Gas 6). Make choux pastry. Sift flour and salt onto a sheet of foil. Combine water and butter in a saucepan. Bring to boil. When butter has melted, remove from heat and add flour, all at once. Stir vigorously to combine.

2 Return pan to heat and stir until mixture forms a ball that leaves the sides of pan clean. Remove from heat and cool for a few minutes.

3 Transfer mixture to a food processor fitted with a plastic blade. With motor running, add eggs one by one, making sure that the first egg has been incorporated completely before adding the next.

4 Pipe marble-sized mounds onto lightly greased baking sheets. Bake for about 30 minutes, until golden and barely moist inside. Cool on a wire rack.

5 To make the avocado filling, combine avocado, lemon juice and onion in a food processor. Process until smooth. Season to taste with salt and cayenne.

6 Cut puffs in half horizontally, slicing them only about three quarters through. Spoon or pipe avocado filling inside. Serve at once.

Makes about 36

Curried Onion Puffs

1 quantity Choux Pastry, see Avocado Puffs left

Curry Filling

30g (1oz) butter

2 onions, finely chopped

2 tspn flour

2 tspn curry powder

125ml (4fl oz) single cream

1 Preheat oven to 200°C (400°F/ Gas 6). Make choux pastry as described in recipe for Avocado Puffs. Place teaspoonfuls of mixture onto lightly greased baking sheets.

2 Bake for 10 minutes, then lower oven temperature to 180°C (350°F/Gas 4) and bake for 10 minutes more or until puffs are crisp and golden brown. Slit puffs to release steam, remove any soft mixture from centre of each and return them to oven to dry out.

3 Meanwhile, make filling. Melt butter in a saucepan, add onion, and cook over gentle heat for about 10 minutes until onion is soft and golden brown. Add flour and curry powder and cook, stirring, for 1 minute. Add cream, stirring until mixture boils and thickens.

4 Spoon a little of the curried onion mixture into each choux puff. Return filled puffs to oven for 10 minutes or until heated through. Serve at once.
Makes about 24

Kitchen Tip
The puffs may be cooked in advance, packed in sealed freezer bags and frozen until required. Thaw in the bags for about 1¹/₂ hours. The puffs may seem rather soft when they are first thawed, but will soon regain their crispness if transferred to baking sheets and cooked in a preheated 180°C (350°F/Gas 4) oven for 5 minutes.

Curried Onion Puffs

Cucumber Puffs

1 quantity Choux Pastry, see Avocado Puffs left

2 medium cucumbers, peeled, seeded and cut into chunks

3 tblspn finely chopped fresh parsley

1 onion, quartered

mayonnaise

salt

freshly ground black pepper

1 Make 36 puffs as described in recipe for Avocado Puffs.

2 Combine cucumber, parsley and onion in a food processor. Process to finely chop.

3 Transfer mixture to a bowl and add enough mayonnaise to make a creamy paste. Add salt and pepper to taste. Fill cold puffs with mixture and serve.
Makes about 36

Spiced Prawn Puffs

1 quantity Choux Pastry, see Avocado Puffs left

125g (4oz) butter

1 tspn ground cumin

¹/₄ tspn ground cardamom

¹/₂ tspn garam masala

185g (6oz) peeled cooked prawns

lemon juice

salt

freshly ground black pepper

1 Make 36 puffs as described in recipe for Avocado Puffs.

2 Melt butter, add spices and cook over low heat for 1 minute.

3 Meanwhile process prawns in a food processor until finely chopped. With motor running, slowly add butter and spice mixture. Blend well.

4 Transfer mixture to a bowl and add lemon juice, salt and pepper to taste. Fill warm puffs with mixture and serve at once.
Makes about 36

SATURDAY SUPPERS

Whether your Saturdays are spent on a squash court, a rugby field or in the supermarket scrum, you'll enjoy coming home to these delicious easy-to-cook supper dishes.

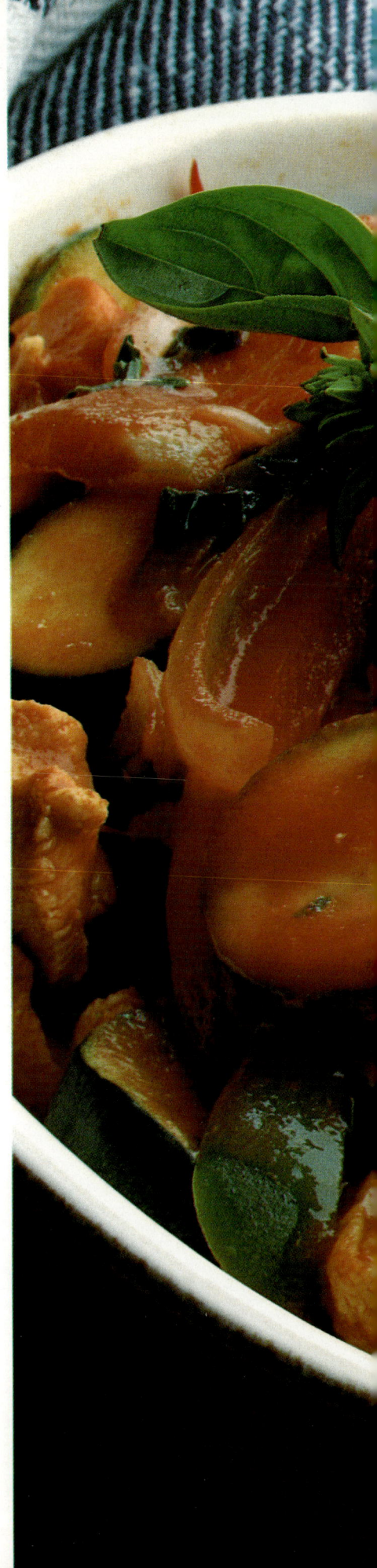

Sausage and Bean Soup

220g (7oz) dried cannellini beans, soaked overnight in water to cover

2 litres (3¹/₂pt) unsalted chicken stock

2 bay leaves

2 sprigs fresh thyme or ¹/₄ tspn dried thyme

2 tblspn olive oil

1 large onion, chopped

2 sticks celery, sliced

¹/₂ red pepper, seeded and chopped

1 tblspn chopped fresh parsley

1 x 410g (13oz) can chopped tomatoes with basil

185ml (6fl oz) passata or puréed tomatoes

2 cloves garlic, chopped

60ml (2fl oz) red wine

6 herby pork sausages

1 Drain beans. Combine them with 1.5 litres (2¹/₂pt) of stock in a large saucepan. Add bay leaves and thyme. Boil for 10 minutes, then simmer for 1 hour or until beans are tender.

2 Heat oil in a large frying pan and sauté onion, celery and pepper for 5 minutes. Stir in parsley, tomatoes, passata, garlic and wine. Heat through, then purée in a blender or food processor. Add to beans, with remaining stock. Simmer for 30 minutes more.

3 Meanwhile, grill sausages until well cooked. Slice them and add them to soup. Heat through. Serve hot.
Serves 4-6

Herbed Chicken and Tomato Casserole

2 tblspn sunflower oil

1 small onion, sliced

1 green pepper, seeded and cut into strips

1 red pepper, seeded and cut into strips

1 courgette, sliced

375ml (12fl oz) passata or puréed tomatoes

1 tblspn chopped fresh basil

1 tblspn chopped fresh parsley

1 tspn chopped fresh thyme

3 x 125g (4oz) chicken breast fillets, skinned and cut into strips

1 Heat oil in a large frying pan over moderate heat. Add onion and cook until transparent.

2 Add peppers and courgette slices and cook for 2-3 minutes. Stir in passata, bring to boil, then lower heat and simmer for 10 minutes. Stir in herbs.

3 Add chicken strips to sauce and cook over moderate heat for 10 minutes or until tender and cooked through. Serve with a fresh basil garnish, if liked.
Serves 4

Herbed Chicken and Tomato Casserole

Paprika Chicken

60g (2oz) butter

2 onions, sliced

185g (6oz) button mushrooms

1 tblspn paprika

1 tblspn white wine vinegar

4 chicken quarters

500ml (16fl oz) chicken stock

375g (12oz) new potatoes

2 tspn cornflour

155ml (5fl oz) soured cream

1 Melt the butter in a large frying pan (an electric frying pan is ideal), add the onions and mushrooms and cook, stirring, until the onions are golden brown. Stir in the paprika and vinegar and cook for 1 minute.

2 Add the chicken quarters to the pan in a single layer. Cook over moderate heat until browned, turning occasionally. Add the stock and bring to the boil. Lower the heat, cover the pan and simmer for about 45 minutes, or until the chicken is tender and cooked through.

3 Meanwhile, boil the potatoes until tender. Drain and add to the chicken. Mix lightly.

4 Mix the cornflour and soured cream in a small bowl. Add the mixture to the pan, stirring until the sauce boils and thickens. Serve at once.
Serves 4

Cheddar Chicken

4 chicken breast fillets, skinned

1 egg, beaten

60g (2oz) each of fresh white breadcrumbs and grated Cheddar cheese

Preheat oven to 180°C (350°F/Gas 4). Dip the chicken breasts in egg, then in the cheese crumb mixture until well coated. Arrange in a lightly greased ovenproof dish. Bake for 30 minutes. Serve with baked jacket potatoes and a green salad.
Serves 4

Paprika Chicken

Sirloin Patties with Gruyére and Tomato

Sirloin Patties with Gruyére and Tomato

500g (1lb) minced sirloin steak

30g (1oz) butter

1 tomato, sliced, each slice quartered

100g (3¹/₂oz) Gruyére cheese, grated

snipped chives and endive for garnish

1 Form the minced steak into four patties, at least 1cm (¹/₂in) thick. Preheat grill.

2 Melt the butter in a large frying pan over moderate heat. Add the patties and cook for 3 minutes on each side.

3 Transfer to the grill pan and top each patty with sliced tomato and cheese. Grill until the cheese melts. Serve at once, garnished with chives and endive.

Serves 4

Seasoned Sausage Ragout

500g (1lb) minced pork or veal

60g (2oz) fresh parsley, finely chopped

60g (2oz) fresh basil, finely chopped

3 tblspn pinenuts, chopped

1 tblspn olive oil

3 cloves garlic, crushed

1 tspn black peppercorns, crushed

185g (6oz) fresh white breadcrumbs

60g (2oz) grated Parmesan cheese

seasoned flour for coating

oil for shallow frying

12 new potatoes, scrubbed

12 shallots, peeled

2 tblspn soy sauce

125ml (4fl oz) lemon juice

250ml (8fl oz) chicken stock

250ml (8fl oz) dry white wine

3 tblspn chopped fresh basil

1 Combine the minced meat, herbs, pinenuts, oil, garlic, pepper, breadcrumbs and cheese in a large bowl. Mix until well combined, then shape into 12 sausages, each about 10cm (4in) in length. Roll the sausages in the seasoned flour in a shallow bowl.

2 Heat the oil in a frying pan. Cook the sausages a few at a time until browned but not cooked through. Drain on paper towels.

3 Arrange the sausages, potatoes and shallots in a deep saucepan. Combine the soy sauce, lemon juice, stock, wine and basil in a jug; mix well and add to the saucepan. Bring to the boil, lower the heat and simmer, covered, for 20 minutes or until the potatoes are tender and the sausages are completely cooked. Serve.

Serves 6

Shepherd's Pie with Crispy Topping

30g (1oz) butter
2 onions, chopped
4 rindless streaky bacon rashers, chopped
1kg (2lb) lean minced beef
1 tblspn Worcestershire sauce
1 tblspn tomato ketchup
¼ tspn ground cloves
salt
freshly ground black pepper
250ml (8fl oz) red wine

Topping

1.5kg (3lb) large potatoes, quartered
90g (3oz) butter
185-250ml (6-8fl oz) milk
grated nutmeg
60g (2oz) fresh breadcrumbs

1 Melt butter in a large flameproof casserole. Add onions and bacon and sauté for about 5 minutes or until onions are golden. Add minced beef and sauté until well browned, breaking up any chunks with a wooden spoon.

2 Stir in Worcestershire sauce, tomato ketchup and cloves, with salt and pepper to taste. Pour in wine, bring to boil, lower heat and simmer, covered, for 40 minutes.

3 Preheat oven to 180°C (350°F/ Gas 4). Make topping. Cook potatoes in a saucepan of boiling salted water until tender. Drain thoroughly. Combine 60g (2oz) of butter with the milk in clean pan. Heat gently until butter melts, return potatoes to pan and mash thoroughly until creamy. Add salt, pepper and nutmeg to taste.

4 Spread cooked mince in a large ovenproof serving dish. Top with mashed potatoes and sprinkle with breadcrumbs. Dot with the remaining butter. Bake for 30 minutes until the topping is golden and crispy. Serve.
Serves 6-8

Chicken and Apple Casserole

1 x 1.5kg (3lb) chicken
1 tblspn oil
1 onion, sliced
1 Granny Smith apple
2 tspn Dijon mustard
2 tspn cornflour
155ml (5fl oz) apple juice
250ml (8floz) chicken stock
125ml (4fl oz) dry white wine
1 tblspn soy sauce
2 tspn Worcestershire sauce
2 tblspn chopped parsley

1 Preheat oven to 180°C (350°F/ Gas 4). Cut chicken into eight portions. Remove skin and visible fat.

2 Heat oil in a large frying pan. Add onion and cook over moderate heat for 5 minutes, stirring occasionally. Peel and core apple, then slice it into pan. Cook until soft.

3 Using a slotted spoon, transfer onion and apple mixture to a casserole. Add chicken to fat remaining in pan and brown lightly all over. Add to casserole.

4 Mix mustard, cornflour and apple juice in a small bowl. Heat stock, wine, soy sauce and Worcestershire sauce in a saucepan, stir in contents of bowl and cook until mixture boils and thickens. Pour into casserole. Add parsley and mix well.

5 Bake casserole, covered, for 1 hour. Serve with brown rice or chunks of wholemeal bread.

Variation
Substitute 250ml (8fl oz) apple cider for the apple juice and white wine, if preferred. Omit the soy sauce and Worcestershire sauce. For a special occasion, flame 2 tblspn Calvados or cognac in a soup ladle and pour it over the chicken in the casserole before adding the sauce.

Pork with Artichokes

Pork with Artichokes

2 tblspn sunflower oil
1 onion, chopped
1 garlic clove, crushed
1/4 tspn coarsley ground black pepper
750g (11/2lb) pork fillet, cubed
1 x 397g (13oz) can peeled tomatoes or chopped tomatoes
125ml (4fl oz) red wine
1 x 425g (131/2oz) can artichoke hearts, drained and halved
2 tblspn chopped fresh parsley

1 Heat oil in a large frying pan. Add onion, garlic and pepper and cook over gentle heat for 5 minutes. Using a slotted spoon, transfer to a bowl.

2 Add pork to pan and sauté for 3 minutes. Drain fat off.

3 Return onion mixture to pan. Add tomatoes and wine, bring to boil, then simmer, covered, for 20 minutes or until pork is cooked. Stir in artichokes and parsley.
Serves 6

Glazed Bacon

1.25kg (21/2lb) boil-in-the-bag bacon collar joint
30g (1oz) butter
3 tblspn soft dark brown sugar
3 tblspn orange marmalade
1 tblspn Dijon mustard
125ml (4fl oz) dry sherry

1 Put bacon joint in a large saucepan with water to cover. Bring to boil, then simmer for 1 hour. Remove from pan, take off wrappings and transfer bacon to a greased roasting tin.

2 Preheat oven to 180°C (350°F/ Gas 4). Melt butter in a saucepan. Add sugar, marmalade, mustard and sherry and cook over moderate heat until sugar melts. Spoon it over bacon. Bake for 30 minutes, basting every 10 minutes. Serve hot or cold.
Serves 6

Baked Cheese Polenta with Spicy Meat Sauce

Herbed Courgette and Lentil Casserole

185g (6oz) red lentils

2 tspn oil

1 large onion, finely chopped

3 sticks celery, sliced

2 tspn sunflower oil

125g (4oz) frozen peas, thawed

250g (8oz) courgettes, sliced

2 tblspn flour

3 tblspn chopped fresh parsley

2 tblspn chopped fresh basil

1 tspn chopped fresh thyme

salt

freshly ground black pepper

lemon juice

1 Rinse lentils under cold running water, drain, then place in a saucepan. Add plenty of water to cover. Bring to boil, lower heat and simmer for about 20 minutes or until the lentils are tender. Drain,

reserving 300ml (10fl oz) of the cooking liquid.

2 Heat oil in a flameproof casserole, add onion and celery and sauté over moderate heat until onion is soft, about 5 minutes. Stir in lentils with peas and courgettes.

3 Stir in flour and cook for 2 minutes, stirring constantly. Add reserved lentil stock, with parsley, basil and thyme. Mix well. Cook for about 15 minutes, or until all vegetables are tender. Season to taste with salt and pepper and sharpen the flavour with a little lemon juice. Serve hot.
Serves 4

Baked Cheese Polenta with Spicy Meat Sauce

750ml (1¼pt) milk

750ml (1¼pt) water

2 tspn salt

315g (10oz) cornmeal

125g (4oz) grated Parmesan cheese

Sauce

15g (½oz) butter

1 onion, chopped

2 cloves garlic, crushed

500g (1lb) minced steak

250ml (8fl oz) dry white wine

2 tblspn tomato purée

1 x 397g (13oz) can chopped tomatoes with basil

1 bay leaf

250ml (8fl oz) passata or puréed tomatoes

2 tblspn Worcestershire sauce

1 Preheat oven to 180°C (350°F/ Gas 4). Line a greased 20cm (8in) loose-bottomed flan tin with foil. Grease the foil.

2 Make sauce. Melt butter in a large saucepan over moderate heat. Add onion and garlic and cook for 3 minutes. Stir in minced steak and brown it on all sides. Add wine and stir over high heat for 10 minutes.

3 Stir in remaining sauce ingredients, lower heat and simmer for 25 minutes, stirring occasionally.

4 Meanwhile, make the polenta. Combine milk and water in a large saucepan. Add salt and bring to boil, then lower heat to a simmer. Very slowly pour cornmeal, in a slow stream, into simmering mixture, stirring rapidly all time. Cook mixture, stirring constantly, for 15 minutes.

5 Remove pan from heat, stir the cheese into polenta mixture and pour into prepared tin. Bake for 20 minutes.

6 Serve polenta in wedges, accompanied by spicy meat sauce.
Serves 6-8

Spanish Chickpea Casserole

500g (1lb) chickpeas, soaked overnight in water to cover

5 tblspn sunflower oil

2 onions, chopped

60g (2oz) pinenuts

375g (12oz) tomatoes, skinned, seeded and chopped

185g (6oz) chorizo or similar spicy sausage, sliced

2 hard-boiled eggs, chopped

1 Drain and rinse chickpeas. Place in a saucepan with water to cover. Bring to boil, lower heat and simmer for 20 minutes. Drain chickpeas, reserving 300ml (10fl oz) of cooking liquid, and place in a casserole.

2 Preheat oven to 160°C (325°F/ Gas 3). Heat oil in a large frying pan. Add onions and cook over moderate heat for 10 minutes, or until golden. Add pinenuts and sauté for 2 minutes.

3 Stir in tomatoes. Cook for 15 minutes or until sauce thickens. Add sausage and cook for 2 minutes.

4 Add mixture to casserole, with salt and pepper to taste. Pour in reserved chickpea stock and mix. Cover casserole and bake for 1½ hours. Sprinkle with hard-boiled egg just before serving.
Serves 4-6

Pasta with Tomato Sauce

2 tblspn oil

1 onion, chopped

3 carrots, grated

1 clove garlic, crushed

2 x 397g (13oz) cans chopped tomato with herbs

500g (1lb) tortellini with cheese filling

60ml (2fl oz) soured cream

grated Parmesan cheese to serve

1 Heat oil in a saucepan, add onion, carrots and garlic and sauté for 5 minutes. Stir in tomatoes. Bring to boil, lower heat and simmer for 20 minutes.

2 Cook tortellini in a large saucepan of boiling water for 8-10 minutes or until tender.

3 Meanwhile, purée tomato mixture in a blender or food processor until smooth. Return to clean saucepan, stir in soured cream and heat through without boiling.

4 Drain tortellini, spoon into individual dishes and pour sauce over top. Serve sprinkled with Parmesan.
Serves 4

Neopolitan Pizza

4 tblspn tomato purée

2 tblspn white wine

1 ready-cooked pizza base

500ml (18fl oz) passata or puréed tomatoes

250g (8oz) mozzarella cheese, sliced

1 x 50g (2oz) can anchovies, drained

1 tspn dried mixed herbs, optional

fresh coriander sprig to garnish

1 Preheat oven to 180°C (350°F/ Gas 4). Mix tomato purée and wine in a small bowl. Spread over pizza base. Spoon passata over pizza and spread out to edges. Top with slices of mozzarella. Arrange anchovies on top of cheese. Add a sprinkling of herbs if liked.

2 Bake pizza for 20 minutes or until cheese has melted and the topping is very hot. Serve at once, with a coriander garnish.
Serves 4

Neopolitan Pizza

Chicken Lasagne

8-10 sheets of lasagne

30g (1oz) butter

2 onions, finely chopped

2 cloves garlic, crushed

6 chicken breast fillets, cut into 5mm (¹/₄in) strips

500g (1lb) broccoli florets

2 sticks celery, sliced

3 tblspn chopped fresh parsley

500g (1lb) mozzarella cheese, thinly sliced

30g (1oz) grated Parmesan cheese

Sauce

75g (2¹/₂oz) butter

30g (1oz) flour

500ml (16fl oz) warm milk

250ml (8fl oz) warm chicken stock

3 eggs

125g (4oz) grated Parmesan cheese

salt

freshly ground black pepper

pinch of grated nutmeg

1 Preheat oven to 180°C (350°F/Gas 4). Make sauce. Melt butter in a saucepan, stir in flour and cook for 1 minute. Whisk in hot milk until smooth. Add chicken stock and cook, stirring, until mixture boils and thickens slightly.

2 Beat eggs in a separate bowl. Add sauce a little at a time, whisking after each addition. Stir in Parmesan, with salt, pepper and nutmeg to taste.

3 Cook lasagne, in boiling salted water until tender. Drain and stand in a bowl of cool water until required.

4 Melt butter in a wok or large frying pan. Add onion and sauté until golden. Add garlic and sauté for 1 minute more. Using a slotted spoon, transfer mixture to a bowl.

5 Add chicken to wok or pan and sauté. Return onion mixture and gently stir in broccoli and celery. Cook, covered, until just tender. Add parsley, with salt and pepper to taste.

6 Spoon a thin layer of sauce onto base of a 35 x 25cm (14 x 10in) large baking dish. Drain and dry lasagne, and arrange a layer on top of sauce. Top with half chicken and broccoli mixture, cover with half remaining sauce. Add half mozzarella slices and a dusting of Parmesan. Repeat layers.

7 Bake for 50 minutes, covering lasagne with foil if topping starts to overbrown towards end of cooking time.

Serves 8

Fettucine with Creamy Pumpkin Sauce

1 pumpkin

500g (1lb) fettucine

500ml (16fl oz) double cream

¹/₄ tspn freshly ground black pepper

¹/₂ tspn ground nutmeg

1 tspn snipped chives

1 Cut 185g (6oz) of pumpkin flesh into strips. Bring a saucepan of water to boil, add strips and cook until just tender. Drain and refresh under cold water. Cube remaining pumpkin flesh and cook in boiling water until tender. Drain and mash. Set aside 185ml (6fl oz) of mashed pumpkin. Use rest in another recipe, such as pumpkin pie.

2 Bring a large saucepan of water to boil, add fettucine and cook until just tender. Drain.

3 Meanwhile heat cream in a deep frying pan until reduced by half. Whisk in reserved mashed pumpkin, with pepper and nutmeg. Gently stir in chives and reserved pumpkin strips. Add fettucine and toss gently to heat through. Serve.

Serves 4

Fettucine with Creamy Pumpkin Sauce

Mushroom Risotto with Italian Sausage Bolognese

60g (2oz) butter

2 onions, finely chopped

250g (8oz) mushrooms, chopped

2 cloves garlic, crushed

220g (7oz) short grain rice

600ml (1pt) chicken stock

1 tblspn olive oil

4 Italian sausages, casings removed

185ml (6fl oz) passata or puréed tomatoes

1 x 397g (13oz) can chopped tomatoes with herbs

salt

freshly ground black pepper

1 Melt butter in a large deep frying pan over moderate heat. Add half the onion and all the mushrooms. Cook for 5 minutes, stirring occasionally. Add garlic and rice, stir well and cook for 2 minutes more.

2 Stir in stock. Bring to boil, lower heat and simmer uncovered for 15 minutes, stirring occasionally, by which time most of the liquid should have been absorbed.

3 Meanwhile, heat the oil in a saucepan over moderate heat. Add the remaining onion with sausagemeat. Cook, stirring, for 7 minutes. Drain off excess oil.

4 Stir in passata and chopped tomatoes, with salt and pepper to taste. Simmer for 7 minutes more.

5 Transfer risotto to a serving dish, top with the sausage bolognese and serve at once.

Serves 4

Kitchen Tips

If the risotto is still very moist towards the end of the cooking time, raise the heat to high for 4-5 minutes. Stir frequently to avoid the rice catching on the base of the pan.

Cumberland sausages may be substituted for Italian sausages, with very good results.

Mushroom Risotto with Italian Sausage Bolognese, Vermicelli with Broccoli and Almonds

3 Drain pasta and add it to sauce with half the grated Parmesan. Toss over heat for 2 minutes. Serve immediately, offering remaining Parmesan separately.
Serves 6

Variation
Stilton may be used instead of Cambozola, if preferred.

Vermicelli with Broccoli and Almonds

440g (14oz) broccoli
60g (2oz) butter
3 tblspn olive oil
2 tblspn finely chopped spring onion
2 cloves garlic, crushed
1 tspn sambal oelek or Tabasco to taste
1/2 tspn coarsely ground black pepper
60g (2oz) flaked almonds
3 tblspn dry white wine
500g (1lb) vermicelli noodles

1 Only broccoli florets are required for this recipe. Reserve stems for a stir fry or similar dish. Bring a saucepan of water to boil, add broccoli florets and blanch for 2 minutes. Drain, refresh under cold water, drain again and set aside.

2 Melt butter with the oil in a large frying pan. Add spring onion, garlic, sambal oelek, pepper and almonds. Cook for 2 minutes over moderate heat. Stir in wine and cook for 3 minutes more. Add broccoli and heat through.

3 Cook vermicelli in a large saucepan of boiling water for 30 seconds or until tender. Drain thoroughly, toss with broccoli mixture and serve at once.
Serves 4

Shell Pasta with Cambozola Sauce

500g (1lb) shell pasta
250g (8oz) Cambozola cheese, diced
300ml (10fl oz) single cream
90g (3oz) butter
salt
freshly ground black pepper
90g (3oz) grated Parmesan cheese

1 Bring a large saucepan of water to the boil. Add the pasta and cook until just tender.

2 Meanwhile make the sauce. Combine Cambozola, cream and butter in a flameproof casserole. Stir over low heat until cheese and butter have melted and sauce is creamy. Season with plenty of black pepper.

Light Bites for Late Nights

Supper is a movable feast. It can be an early evening meal with the children, an eight o'clock casserole to revive flagging spirits or a simple repast shared with friends after a trip to the theatre or cinema. These recipes cater for the final category.

Pasta Primavera

salt

60g (2oz) broccoli florets

60g (2oz) cauliflower florets

1 courgette, thinly sliced

1 small carrot, cut diagonally into thin slices

500g (1lb) spaghetti

1 tblspn olive oil

2 spring onions, thinly sliced

1 small tomato, chopped

1/2 green pepper, chopped

1 small jar prepared pesto sauce

125g (4oz) prosciutto, cut into thin strips

grated Parmesan cheese to serve

1 Bring 1 medium and 1 large saucepan of lightly salted water to the boil.

2 Blanch the broccoli, cauliflower, courgette and carrot in boiling water in medium pan for 2 minutes. Drain, refresh under cold water and drain again.

3 Cook spaghetti in larger pan until just tender.

4 Meanwhile, heat oil in a frying pan. Add drained vegetables with spring onions, tomato and green pepper. Stir fry for 4 minutes, or until vegetables are crisp-tender.

5 Drain pasta and place in a large heated bowl. Add vegetable mixture with pesto and prosciutto. Toss to mix. Serve immediately, offering Parmesan separately.
Serves 4

Fettucine with Red Pepper and Goats' Cheese

410g (13oz) fettucine

2 tblspn oil

2 cloves garlic, crushed

2 red peppers, cut into thin strips

8 spring onions, cut into thin strips

1/2 tspn coarsely ground black pepper

10g (3 1/2oz) goats' cheese, crumbled

1 Bring a large saucepan of water to the boil. Add the fettucine and cook until just tender.

2 Meanwhile heat the oil in a large deep frying pan over moderate heat. Add the garlic and red peppers and cook for 2 minutes, taking care not to allow the garlic to burn. Add the spring onions and black pepper and cook for 1 minute more.

3 Drain the pasta and add to the red pepper mixture. Toss well. Carefully stir in the cheese.

4 Divide the pasta between four serving dishes. Serve at once.
Serves 4

Fettucine with Red Pepper and Goats' Cheese

Buckwheat Noodles Puttanesca

1 x 397g (13oz) can chopped tomatoes

10 green stuffed olives, sliced

1 tblspn chopped fresh basil

1 tblspn chopped spring onions

10 capers, drained

185g (6oz) dry buckwheat noodles

4 fresh basil sprigs for garnish

1 Combine the tomatoes, olives, basil, spring onions and capers in a medium saucepan. Bring the mixture to the boil over moderate heat, then simmer for 15 minutes.

2 Cook the noodles in a large saucepan of boiling salted water until just tender. Drain thoroughly.

3 Divide noodles between serving plates. Top with a tomato sauce. Serve garnished with basil sprigs.

Serves 4

Spaghetti with Olives and Peperoni

410g (13oz) spaghetti

2 tblspn olive oil

30g (1oz) black olives, pitted and chopped

100g (3½ oz) slices peperoni, chopped

1 onion, finely chopped

fresh basil for garnish

1 Cook the spaghetti in a large saucepan of boiling salted water until just tender.

2 Meanwhile, heat oil in a large deep frying pan. Add the olives, peperoni and onion and cook for about 5 minutes or until the onion is transparent.

3 Drain spaghetti and add it to frying pan. Toss well. Divide between serving plates and serve, garnished with basil.

Serves 4

Kitchen Tip

This is delicious served with a salad made by mixing blanched cauliflower florets with shredded anchovy fillets, green olives and capers, lightly tossed with olive oil and lemon juice.

Fettucine with Creamy Avocado Sauce

500g (1lb) fettucine

salt

2 ripe avocados, halved, stoned and peeled

2 cloves garlic, crushed

1 tblspn lemon juice

3 tblspn roughly chopped fresh basil

125ml (4fl oz) water

freshly ground black pepper

30g (1oz) butter

250ml (8fl oz) single cream

1 Cook fettucine in a large saucepan of boiling salted water until just tender.

2 Meanwhile purée avocados with garlic, lemon juice, basil and water in a food processor, stopping at least once to scrape down sides. Add salt and pepper to taste.

3 Melt butter in a heavy saucepan. Add avocado mixture and heat through over moderate heat, stirring constantly. Add cream and cook for about 3 minutes, until the sauce thickens.

4 Drain cooked pasta, divide it between serving plates. Pour sauce over. Serve.

Serves 4

Spaghetti with Olives and Peperoni, served with a cauliflower salad

Rigatoni with Smoked Turkey and Ricotta

500g (1lb) rigatoni

salt

1 tblspn oil

375g (12oz) smoked turkey, finely chopped

125g (4oz) ricotta cheese

30g (1oz) grated Parmesan cheese

2 eggs, beaten

3 tblspn chopped fresh basil

1 tblspn chopped fresh oregano

freshly ground black pepper

500ml (16fl oz) chicken stock

Tomato and Oregano Sauce

125ml (4fl oz) olive oil

1/2 onion, finely chopped

4 cloves garlic, crushed

2kg (4lb) tomatoes, skinned, seeded and chopped

250ml (8fl oz) red wine

3 tblspn oregano leaves

1 tblspn tomato purée

Garnish

diced red, green and yellow peppers

2 tblspn chopped fresh parsley

Spaghetti Carbonara

1 Cook the rigatoni in a large saucepan of salted water until just tender, adding the oil to the water to prevent the pasta from sticking. Drain.

2 Combine the turkey, ricotta, Parmesan, eggs, basil and oregano in a bowl. Mix well and add salt and pepper to taste. Stuff each pasta tube with about 1¹/₂ teaspoons of the mixture. Place on a baking sheet lined with nonstick baking parchment. Cover and refrigerate.

3 Make sauce. Heat oil in a large saucepan over moderate heat. Sauté onion for 2 minutes, then add garlic and sauté for 1 minute more. Add tomatoes, wine, oregano and tomato purée. Bring to boil, lower heat and simmer for about 20 minutes or until thickened. Add salt and pepper to taste.

4 Heat chicken stock in a large saucepan. Add the rigatoni; simmer for about 5 minutes or until heated through.

5 Spoon sauce onto heated plates. Top with rigatoni and garnish with chopped peppers and parsley.
Serves 6

Spaghetti Carbonara

500g (1lb) spaghetti

salt

1 tblspn olive oil

375g (12oz) lean cooked ham, cut into thin strips

4 eggs

60ml (2fl oz) single cream

90g (3oz) grated Pecorino cheese

1 Cook spaghetti in a large saucepan of boiling salted water until just tender.

2 Meanwhile heat the olive oil gently in a frying pan, add ham and heat through.

3 In a large heated bowl, beat eggs with cream and Pecorino.

4 Drain cooked spaghetti and immediately toss it with egg and cheese mixture so that heat of the pasta 'cooks' the sauce.

5 Add the ham and toss again. Serve at once.
Serves 4

Eggs Benedicta

6 thick slices wholemeal bread

15g (1/2oz) butter, softened

2 heads chicory, finely sliced

6 slices smoked salmon

6 eggs

Hollandaise Sauce (recipe follows)

1 tblspn chopped dill

2 tblspn red lumpfish roe

1 Cut bread into rounds and spread very thinly with butter. Place on serving plates.

2 Cover each round with a thin layer of sliced chicory. Top with a slice of smoked salmon.

3 Poach eggs gently. Meanwhile make Hollandaise sauce. Drain eggs, trim whites and place one egg on each smoked salmon slice.

4 Pour hot Hollandaise sauce over. Garnish each portion with chopped dill and red lumpfish roe.
Serves 6

Hollandaise Sauce

250g (8oz) butter

3 egg yolks

1 tblspn water

2-3 tblspn lemon juice

salt

freshly ground black pepper

pinch cayenne pepper

1 Melt butter in a small saucepan over gentle heat; do not brown. Combine egg yolks, water and 2 tablespoons of lemon juice in a blender or food processor. With motor running, gradually add the foaming butter through feeder tube in a steady stream. The sauce will thicken.

2 Add salt and pepper to taste, sharpening flavour with lemon juice if necessary. Blend for a few seconds longer. This sauce can be kept warm in the top of a double boiler.
Makes about 375ml (12fl oz)

Piperade

1 tblspn olive oil

2 green peppers, seeded and cut into short strips

2 leeks, white part only, finely chopped

1 onion, finely chopped

2 ripe tomatoes, diced

155g (5oz) lean cooked ham, chopped

3 tblspn chopped fresh parsley

3 eggs

125ml (4fl oz) milk

1 Preheat oven to 180°C (350°F/ Gas 4). Heat oil in a large frying pan over moderate heat. Add the pepper strips, leeks and onion and cook for 3 minutes, stirring occasionally.

2 Add tomatoes and ham and cook for 5 minutes. Stir in parsley and remove pan from heat.

3 Beat eggs and milk together, add to vegetable mixture and mix well.

4 Pour mixture into a greased 23cm (9in) flan dish. Bake for 30 minutes or until cooked through. Serve at once.
Serves 6

Kitchen Tip
If preferred, piperade may be cooked on top of the stove. Simply add the egg mixture to the frying pan and cook as for a Spanish omelette.

Salmon Frittata

Salmon Frittata

30g (1oz) butter

1 onion, finely chopped

2 spring onions, finely chopped

½ green pepper, seeded and finely chopped

1 leek, white part only, thinly sliced

1 tomato, diced

155g (5oz) smoked salmon, chopped

4 eggs

185ml (6fl oz) milk

freshly ground black pepper

1 Melt the butter in a frying pan. Add the onion, spring onions, pepper and leek slices; cook over moderate heat for 4-5 minutes until softened but not browned.

2 Add the tomato and salmon. Cook for 1 minute, then remove the pan from the heat and allow the mixture to cool to room temperature.

3 Preheat oven to 180°C (350°F/ Gas 4). Beat the eggs and milk in a bowl, adding plenty of black pepper to taste. Stir into the cooled salmon and vegetable mixture.

4 Pour the mixture into a greased 20cm (8in) flan dish and bake for 25 minutes or until cooked through. Serve at once.
Serves 6

Kitchen Tips
Frittatas are ideal late supper dishes. The basic mixture can be varied to suit the contents of your vegetable rack and storecupboard; canned salad-cut asparagus is an excellent addition, as are quartered artichoke hearts. Any smoked fish can be substituted for the salmon in the recipe above; trout is delicious. Alternatively, use ham, crumbled grilled bacon or sliced frankfurters. For a vegetarian version, substitute 185g (6oz) sliced mushrooms for the salmon. Serve with a simple watercress, cucumber and walnut salad to add extra colour and a contrast in texture.

Chicken with Apples and Onions

45g (1½oz) butter

4 chicken breast fillets, skinned and cut into 2cm (¾in) squares

2 red eating apples, sliced

1 large red onion, sliced

4 sticks celery, sliced

60ml (2fl oz) freshly squeezed orange juice

60ml (2fl oz) apple juice

freshly ground black pepper

250ml (8fl oz) single cream

1 Melt butter in a large saucepan over moderate heat. Add chicken, apples, onion and celery and cook, stirring, for 3 minutes.

2 Add orange juice, apple juice and pepper. Bring to boil, then lower heat and simmer for 5 minutes.

3 Stir in cream and cook over high heat without boiling for 5 minutes or until sauce thickens slightly and chicken is cooked.
Serves 4

Lime Rum Chicken

1 x 1.5kg (3lb) chicken, cut into 4cm (1½in) pieces

3 limes

185ml (6fl oz) white rum

60ml (2fl oz) soy sauce

2 garlic cloves, crushed

flour for dredging

oil for deep frying

1 Place chicken in a bowl. Squeeze juice from two limes, add to chicken and toss lightly.

2 Combine rum, soy sauce and crushed garlic in a small bowl. Pour over chicken and mix well. Cover and refrigerate for at least 5 hours, preferably overnight.

3 Drain chicken pieces; dredge in flour. Deep fry for 5 minutes, turning once, until golden. Drain. Serve with remaining lime wedges.
Serves 4

Chicken Piccata

4 chicken breast fillets, skinned

flour for dredging

60g (2oz) butter

250ml (8fl oz) dry vermouth

125ml (4fl oz) chicken stock

4 tblspn chopped fresh parsley

2 tblspn drained capers

lemon slices for garnish

1 Put chicken breasts between sheets of greaseproof paper and flatten with a mallet or rolling pin. Cut into thin strips. Dredge in flour, shaking off excess.

2 Melt butter in a heavy-based frying pan. Add chicken and toss over moderate heat for 1-2 minutes to brown. Add vermouth, stock and parsley, with salt and pepper to taste.

3 Lower heat and simmer until the chicken is cooked. Serve garnished with capers and lemon slices.
Serves 4

Herbed Chicken in Foil

4 chicken breast fillets, skinned

4 tblspn chopped fresh herbs

125ml (4fl oz) lemon juice

1 small onion, very thinly sliced, rings separated

75g (2½oz) butter

1 Preheat oven to 190°C (375°F/ Gas 5). Place each chicken breast on a piece of foil large enough to enclose it completely.

2 Sprinkle each chicken breast with 1 tablespoon of the herbs, 2 tablespoons of lemon juice and a few onion rings. Dot each portion with butter; add salt and pepper to taste. Bring up the foil to make loose but secure parcels.

3 Bake for 30-40 minutes, until chicken is cooked.
Serves 4

Double Chicken Burgers

500g (1lb) minced chicken

1 egg, lightly beaten

30g (1oz) fresh white breadcrumbs

2 tspn Worcestershire sauce

45g (1½oz) butter

4 hamburger buns

1 Combine minced chicken, egg, breadcrumbs and Worcestershire sauce in a bowl; mix well. Mould mixture into eight patties.

2 Fry patties in melted butter in a frying pan until golden, pressing patties down with a spatula, and allowing about 3 minutes per side. Drain on paper towels. Serve two patties in each hamburger bun, separating them with a small salad if liked.
Serves 4

Chicken with Creamy Tarragon Sauce

45g (1½oz) butter

4 chicken breast fillets, skinned

1 tblspn finely chopped fresh tarragon

1 tblspn Dijon mustard

185ml (6fl oz) dry white wine

250ml (8fl oz) single cream

1 Preheat oven to 110°C (225°F/ Gas ¼).Melt butter in a large frying pan over moderate heat. Add chicken to pan and cook until golden on both sides. Continue to cook over low heat until chicken is just cooked. Transfer to a baking dish and keep warm in oven.

2 Add tarragon, mustard and wine to pan and boil until reduced by half.

3 Add cream and cook until mixture boils and thickens slightly. Pour over chicken fillets and serve at once
Serves 4

Chicken with Apple and Onions (top), Chicken with Creamy Tarragon Sauce

Vegetable Stir Fry

1 tblspn sunflower oil
1 clove garlic, crushed
1 tspn grated ginger
½ tspn sesame oil
1 bunch asparagus, trimmed, cut into diagonal lengths
125g (4oz) green beans, cut into diagonal lengths
1 carrot, cut into diagonal slices
1 red pepper, seeded and cut into diamonds

1 Preheat a wok or large frying pan. Add sunflower oil. When hot, add garlic, ginger and sesame oil. Cook for 30 seconds.

2 Add vegetables and stir fry for 3 minutes or until crisp-tender. Serve at once, with noodles or brown rice if liked.

Serves 4

Vegetable Stir Fry

Gingered Potato Pancakes

3 large potatoes
3 eggs, lightly beaten
1 tblspn grated fresh root ginger
salt
freshly ground black pepper
oil for shallow frying

1 Grate peeled potatoes roughly into a sieve. Using a wooden spoon, press potatoes against side of sieve to extract as much liquid as possible.

2 Transfer potato to a bowl and add eggs and ginger. Stir well. Add salt and pepper to taste.

3 Pour oil to a depth of about 5mm (¼in) into a large frying pan. Carefully drop generous tablespoonfuls of potato mixture into hot oil; flatten each round with back of the spoon to make a 7.5cm (3in) pancake.

4 Fry over moderately high heat for about 5 minutes until browned underneath, then turn pancakes over and brown other side for about 4 minutes. Drain on paper towels, then pile the pancakes onto a platter and keep warm while cooking the rest of the mixture. Serve hot.

Serves 4

Fennel Fricassee

3 small fennel bulbs, trimmed
12 shallots, peeled but left whole
4 large potatoes, cut into 2cm (¾in) cubes
250g (8oz) thickly sliced bacon, cubed
45g (1½oz) butter
salt
freshly ground black pepper
60-125ml (2-4fl oz) chicken stock
1 clove garlic, crushed
2 tblspn finely chopped fresh parsley

1 Bring a small saucepan of salted water to the boil. Cut fennel into quarters and cook in boiling water for 5 minutes or until tender. Using a slotted spoon, transfer to paper towels to drain.

2 Bring water to boil again, add shallots and potato cubes and cook for 5 minutes. Drain and set aside.

3 Refill the clean pan with water, bring to the boil and add the bacon. Boil for 1 minute, then drain and dry thoroughly on paper towels.

4 Melt the butter in a frying pan. Add the bacon cubes and sauté over moderate to high heat until crisp. Drain on paper towels.

5 Add the shallots and potato cubes to the frying pan; sauté until the potato starts to brown. Add salt and pepper to taste.

6 Add the fennel to the pan, with 60ml (2fl oz) of the stock. Cover the pan and cook for 5 minutes, adding more stock if necessary. Add the bacon and cook until heated through. Stir in the garlic and parsley; cook for 30 seconds more. Serve at once.

Serves 4

Useful Information

Length

Centimetres	Inches	Centimetres	Inches
0.5 (5mm)	$1/4$	18	7
1	$1/2$	20	8
2	$3/4$	23	9
2.5	1	25	10
4	$1^1/2$	30	12
5	2	35	14
6	$2^1/2$	40	16
7.5	3	45	18
10	4	50	20
15	6	NB: 1cm = 10 mm	

Metric/Imperial Conversion Chart

Mass (Weight)
(Approximate conversions for cookery purposes)

Metric	Imperial	Metric	Imperial
15g	$1/2$oz	315g	10oz
30g	1oz	350g	11oz
60g	2oz	375g	12oz ($3/4$lb)
90g	3oz	410g	13oz
125g	4oz ($1/4$lb)	440g	14oz
155g	5oz	470g	15oz
185g	6oz	500g (0.5kg)	16oz (1lb)
220g	7oz	750g	24oz ($1^1/2$lb)
250g	8oz ($1/2$lb)	1000g (1kg)	32oz (2lb)
280g	9oz	1500 (1.5kg)	3lb

Metric Spoon Sizes

$1/4$ teaspoon	= 1.25ml
$1/2$ teaspoon	= 2.5ml
1 teaspoon	= 5ml
1 tablespoon	=15ml

Liquids

Metric	Imperial
30ml	1fl oz
60 ml	2fl oz
90ml	3fl oz
125ml	4fl oz
155ml	5fl oz ($1/4$pt)
185ml	6fl oz
250ml	8fl oz
500ml	16fl oz
600ml	20fl oz (1pt)
750ml	$1^1/4$pt
1 litre	$1^3/4$pt
1.2 litres	2pt
1.5 litres	$2^1/2$pt
1.8 litres	3pt
2 litres	$3^1/2$pt
2.5 litres	4pt

Index

Editorial Coordination: Merehurst Limited
Cookery Editor: Jenni Fleetwood
Editorial Assistant: Sheridan Packer
Production Manager: Sheridan Carter
Layout and Finished Art: Stephen Joseph
Cover Photography: David Gill
Cover Design: Maggie Aldred
Cover Home Economist: Maxine Clark
Cover Stylist: Hilary Guy

Published by J.B. Fairfax Press Pty Limited
80-82 McLachlan Avenue
Rushcutters Bay 2011
A.C.N. 003 738 430

Formatted by J.B. Fairfax Press Pty Limited
Printed by Toppan Printing Co, Singapore

JBFP 315 A/UK
Includes Index
ISBN 1 86343 116 0 (set)
ISBN 1 86343 154 3

Distribution and Sales Enquires
Australia: J.B. Fairfax Press Pty Limited
Ph: (02) 361 6366 Fax: (02) 360 6262
United Kingdom: J.B. Fairfax Press Limited
Ph: (0933) 402330 Fax (0933) 402234